First Printing: April 2020
ISBN 978-0-578-68685-1
I'Jale Publishing Co. LLC

The Money Manual
(All things Taxes)

Written By: Shondricka Carter

KJALE™
PUBLISHING CO.

The Money Table of Contents

Introduction:
Ultimate Guide for New Tax Preparers
Building a Tax Preparation Business

Benjamin Franklin wrote, "Nothing can be said to be certain, except death and taxes." It's only logical that if you were to build a business, being in the tax industry is a stable choice.

Over the years, the Internal Revenue Service upgraded its processes and systems which paved the way for the growth of the tax industry. It also led to the practice of tax preparation that started in the 1980s.

Complications in tax procedures urged individuals and businesses to seek assistance from tax professionals. In 2019, 56% or 71,725,000 of e-Filed tax returns were done by tax professionals.

IRS allows professionals who are registered with them to file tax returns for their clients. Tax professionals are Tax Preparers, Enrolled Agents, Certified Public Accountants (CPAs), and Attorneys.

Since 2000, becoming a tax preparer has been a lucrative career. The top five states with most tax preparers are from California, Texas, Florida, New York, and Illinois.

We started our tax company Carter Capital, PLLC in 2013. Shondricka Carter Carter Capital, PLLC with a passion for numbers and an extensive financial background. Every year the client base grew and the services enhanced. Shondricka learned how to make money work best for small businesses developing strategies while bootstrapping and how to become a scalable profitable small business.

Tax preparation is an annual-type of work. Busy season is from January to April of each year. Aside from registered tax preparers, most tax-related businesses such as accounting or law firms expand their services to tax preparation.

Every year, people undergo training to become a tax preparer. They also register, and start their own business or get employed.

Overall, the IRS issued 773,911 Preparer Tax Identification Numbers (PTINs) and 360,000 offices registered with Electronic Filing Identification Numbers (EFINs) for the year 2019.

Building a tax preparation business is easy. It has minimal start-up costs and a high return. It's also a stable career. If you're just graduated from high school and want to start a career in finance, becoming a tax preparer can be your first step.

In 2019, we launched Carter and Associates, LLC a tax preparation company. The two worked tirelessly to create a new kind of business model – one that replaced compromise with a sense of achievement.

Building became effortless for us, so we thought, why stop there?
Today Bruce and Shondricka Carter (Carter And Associates, LLC) have built a team in less than three months served over 260 clients within the 50 states that grossed over $100,000 in its first year. Now we are helping tax preparers grow their businesses the same way we grew ours. We are more than your average tax office.

To help individuals more easily become business owners we created tools that balance the money for everyday expenses with near-future and long-term goals. And because we're rooted in innovative business practices, we're launching avenues that help people get even more happiness from every dollar spent and saved.

Chapter 1: What are the responsibilities of a Tax Preparer?

Tax preparers are responsible for filing federal and state tax returns for clients. They should be an expert in all types of tax forms appropriate for their clients' needs. Also, they are knowledgeable about schedules set by the IRS.

Clients of tax preparers range from individuals to business owners. Individuals hire tax preparers to work on their personal tax returns. While business owners hire them to manage business returns such as Corporations and Partnerships. Business tax returns are more complicated. It involves accounting or bookkeeping to make sure all records are correct before filing tax returns.

Starting your career as a tax preparer is not difficult. Tax preparers do not need to get professional licenses. However, they should register for a PTIN with the IRS. You can also become an Enrolled Agent (EA). This would allow you to represent clients before the IRS.

Carter Capital offers training for beginners & experienced tax professionals. There's no need to be accredited, but having the certificate helps to get hired or get paid more.

Once you've finished your training and registered with the IRS, you can start working as a tax preparer. Here's a better look at the responsibilities of being a tax preparer:

Identifying clients' tax needs

Tax preparers are responsible for filing tax forms based on their client's needs. As a tax preparer, you must understand a client's financial situation. You must conduct interviews with your clients to assess their tax preparation needs. Tax programs have interview modes to help you get the information you need from your clients.

Clients would disclose each of their financial activities. So, tax preparers need to be trustworthy. Remember: a tax preparer deal with clients' financial data. Your success in the tax preparation business relies on your integrity and trustworthiness.

Tax preparers should also provide tax information to their clients. It is also common for you to offer advice on completing a client's tax return. Offering advice may not be tax planning, but the basics of tax planning are to make sure the clients' withholdings are correct.

Answering your clients' tax questions are also expected. In some cases, tax preparers offer help with a client's future tax planning. Help clients understand state and federal tax laws to make better financial decisions.

Interviewing the Client

The tax preparation business is not just processing your client's data. It's a business built on good professional relationships. The first chance in building a good relationship with the client is via the tax preparation interview.

Maximize building relationships with your clients with these tips: Make a good first impression

Clients look for tax preparers they can trust. Make sure to communicate this from the very first time you meet your client. Look professional and presentable. Smile and be accommodating. Offer a beverage to your client and make them feel comfortable.

Start asking about your client's personal information first

Before asking your clients about their financial records, start discussing personal information first. Every tax interview starts getting basic information such as full name, birthdates, contact information, occupation, and Social Security numbers.

Ask about your client's previous tax filings

Make the most of your tax preparation interview by understanding your client's previous tax filings. This is a very essential action for when you have new clients. Do your best to get all the data from previous tax years; you'll need to know Adjusted Gross Income to file the tax returns electronically. If your client has been with you already, make sure to check your previous records, too. Looking at your client's previous tax filings might refresh your mind to ask pertinent questions.

Learn about your client's possible incomes

Get to know all of your client's possible sources of income. Some clients do not know that their side business needs to be filed. Knowing about odd jobs or overlooked sources of income would help you advise your client better.

Overlooked sources of income include:
State refunds (when taxable)
Social security
Unemployment benefits

Sometimes, your client may forget about other sources of income when it's a passive income. Examples of those are income from investments. Here's a list of all other sources of income that you need to ask about:

1. Interest Income - investments from a savings account or (certificate of deposit)
2. Dividend Income - income earned from stock or investments
3. Self-Employment Income - income from any job hired that requires 1065 form
4. Sales Commissions
5. Pension Retirement Income
6. IRA or 401(k) Distribution Income
7. Gambling or Lottery Winnings - filed under form W-2G
8. Alimony Income - financial support from a former spouse
9. Rental Income
10. Sale of Business Assets - any sale that happened within the year for tax return filing
11. Sale of Personal Residence - any sale that happened within the year for tax return filing

12. Stock and Bond Sales - any sale that happened within the year for tax return filing

13. Income from Partnerships, Corporations, Trusts, Estates

Some clients forget the income they receive in a year unless asked. So, make sure to be thorough in asking for these details.

Identify any deductions or credits for your client

Asking about any possible deductions or credits for your client helps them get a refund. Go through a list to help jog your client's memory on whether he qualifies for a deduction.

Here are some of the possible tax deductions or credits:

Sales tax
Insurance premiums
Tax savings for Teachers
Charitable gifts
Lifetime learning credit
Unusual business expenses
Unemployment credit
Childcare expenses
Traditional IRA contributions

Help your clients recall through the interview, so you won't miss out on any possible tax deductions. Know all about possible tax credits for your individuals and businesses from the IRS website.

Start tax planning

Once you're done with the interview, get the necessary financial data and start discussing tax planning with your client.

Remember, the tax business is more than just entering data into a computer program. Tax preparers need to understand what the data is representing. Only through understanding your client's insights and data can you serve him better.

Collating financial documents

Tax preparers should collect a client's financial records. Tax preparation entails making sense of the client's finances based on available information.

Types of financial documents clients would submit:

Personal Information
Social Security Number
Tax ID
Birth Date
Income and Investment Information
Form W-2 Wage
Tax Statement
Bank Statements
Last year's refund amount
Miscellaneous income records
Form 1099s
Self-Employment and Business Records (if applicable)
Business Expenses Records
Quarterly Estimated Tax Payment
Mileage Records
Home Office Expenses
Deductibles
Unreimbursed medical expenses receipts
Health Insurance Coverage forms (Form 1095)
Social Security benefits
Charitable Donation receipts
Property Tax receipts

Some clients will submit organized financial documents. Others have all their receipts in a shoebox. You must go through them and identify which ones go on the forms. The more questions you ask your clients, the better information you get. Understanding the information helps you make an accurate representation of your client's tax returns.

Encourage clients to complete these documents to file their tax returns. It will also maximize clients' refunds.

Computes and prepares tax returns

A tax preparer calculates tax returns based on the collated financial documents. You must have excellent attention to detail and technical know-how.

The computations must be error-free because mistakes can incur penalties. Reliable, professional tax software can help compute clients' taxes. Ultimate Tax provides more than just a secure tax software. They provide excellent tax preparer support, too.

You can contact UltimateTax through phone, email, chat, Facebook, and fax. Tax preparers can have peace of mind even when there are difficulties with understanding the program.

Completing client's tax forms

Then, a tax preparer completes the clients' tax forms and files them. You must check each data input and verify computations before filing.

File tax returns either electronically or manually via mail. A tax preparation business must become an IRS affiliate to file electronically. Apply for your Electronic Filing Identification Number (EFIN).

Filing returns electronically is an advantage for both tax preparers and clients. Tax preparers could file returns with faster processing times. You can also reduce inaccuracies on a client's tax return. Clients can also receive their refunds faster.

Clients who would like to file their returns through the mail may do so, as well. The clients would sign a waiver to file taxes electronically.

Offer other products related to tax

Based on a client's needs, tax preparers may offer bank products. Bank products are an additional way for you to add revenue. You can guide and advise their clients on which products to use based on your client's refund amount. Keep in mind that the cheapest and quickest way for clients to get their refunds filed is to get a direct deposit from the IRS.

Tax preparers must be pre-approved before offering bank products to their clients. Get the necessary approvals first to offer these product options.

What type of services should I offer?

Tax Filing
Tax preparers can start a business focus on the filing of taxes. Tax season begins from January to April of the next calendar year. If you extend personal tax returns you have until October to get the returns filed. From December of the previous year, a tax preparer can start providing services to the following clients:

Employed clients
Tax preparers can help with the filing of income tax returns for working clients. Mainly, they can charge for the preparation of clients' W-2 forms.

Corporations
Taxes of corporations and companies are also a good market for the tax filing service. Tax preparers can handle tax filing for small companies to big businesses. However, you may want to consider specializing if this is the type of market you want to get into. For example, you can specialize in tax filing of business in the food industry like restaurants or food suppliers. Handling too many clients from different sectors may be complicated for someone who is just starting. Once you're ready to expand, you can consider branching out to other industries. You can also offer filing 1099s for small

businesses. Each business is required to file 1099s to any supplier that they paid more than $600 in the tax year.

Non-profits

Another type of clients are non-profit organizations. When filing taxes for these types of clients, a particular specialization is also required. Different tax rules apply to non-profit clients. Plus, various exemptions depend on the state where the non-profit organization operates.

Accounting services

Aside from tax filing, tax preparation businesses can also offer accounting services. In some states, you must be a certified public accountant (CPA). In other states, you can offer bookkeeping services which include reconciling and verifying bank statements and items.

Bookkeeping services

Tax preparers have available time for other ventures after the tax season. During the off-season, you can offer bookkeeping services to your clients. Your client's advantage in using your bookkeeping services is that once tax season comes in, it will be easy for you to prepare their taxes. Additionally, since bookkeeping can be a monthly service you can keep income coming in all year long.

Specialized services

The standard tax preparation services are those related to a client's income and investment portfolios. However, there are other dedicated taxes, such as insurance or sales taxes. If you have other qualifications (i.e., you are a lawyer or a CPA), you can also provide this service for your new business.

What clients should I get?

As shared earlier, clients for tax preparation ranges from individuals to business owners. Everyone needs to file taxes. So, there's no shortage of possible clients.

Family and Friends

As a new tax preparer, your family and friends would be your first clients. Ask for their support by being your client. They can help spread awareness of your practice through word-of-mouth and online reviews. Market yourself as the "Tax Guy or Gal."

Connect with your friends who own small businesses. Talk to your former employers and ask around if they would need your services.

Tax preparers need to build trust with their clients. So, it's okay if you've already had a previous connection or relationship with your first ones.

Referrals

Once your family and friends become your client, you'll also receive referrals from them. But you shouldn't stop there. A tax preparer should network and get referrals from your circle of influence.

Get referrals from your suppliers and vendors, former co-workers, and past classmates. Ask references from the members of your organizations and church. Your good relationship with them would be a testament to your future clients.

Another great referral would be from your previous clients, as well. Always put your best foot forward when providing your tax preparation services. A kind word from your past clients is good marketing for your practice. Paying for referrals is also a good business practice. Paying a referral fee of $20 to your client is the best $20 you will spend in advertising.

Local Businesses

Local businesses like restaurants and contractors usually have one to ten employees. Most likely, a bookkeeper would not be one of them. These businesses would outsource tax preparation tasks.

Businesses with accountants and bookkeepers may also outsource tax preparation tasks. Outsourcing tax preparation is an excellent cost-cutting technique. It saves time and money for the company.

Now, that you've learned what kind of services to offer and clients to pursue, start building your own tax preparation business. It is not easy, but it is stable and very profitable. Learn more about how to grow your business.

Chapter 2: The Fundamentals for Tax Preparers

Now that you've identified what services you would like to focus on and built an initial client list, the next step is to work on the necessary registration for your practice. Getting this registration done is mandatory for you to start your professional tax preparer career.

Get your Employer Identification Number (EIN)

Employer Identification Number or EIN is issued for tax administration purposes of your business. An EIN is also known as the Federal Tax Identification Number. Before you can request for other government documents, you would need to process this first. All other government forms will require you to declare your EIN.

TIP: Do not confuse the EIN with your EFIN. These are two separate and different ID numbers. To lessen your confusion, EIN is a 9-digit number while the EFIN is only a 6-digit number.

3 Steps in EIN Application:

Check if you are eligible to apply for an EIN

You can only apply for an EIN if your business located in the U.S.A. or in U.S. territories. Also, you should be eligible to work in the U.S. In this case, you would need to provide your taxpayer information such as your Social Security Number (SSN) and Individual Taxpayer Identification Number (ITIN).

Understand the Online Application

Read the application instructions first before starting your online application. The online application does not have a save option. You must complete this in one session. If you take too long, more than 15 minutes, your application will expire and you have to start over.

Submit application

Once you've finished the application and all validations are done, you will immediately get your EIN. A notice will pop-up, which you can download, save, or print.

Get your Business License or Permit

Business licenses and permits depending on your business type and location. It's best to research what kind of licenses and permits you need in your State. Requirements and fees may also vary.

TIP: Some states issue a license or permit for a limited time only. Make sure to check your documents so you know when you need to renew them.

Get your PTIN

Before you can do work as a tax preparer, you would need to register with the IRS. In this case, you need to get your Preparer Tax Identification Number or most known as PTIN. Getting a PTIN is easy and free. Check out how to get your PTIN here.

Get your EFIN

Nowadays, tax filings are done electronically. In this case, the IRS has required each tax preparation business to get an Electronic Filing Identification Number or EFIN. If you were building your own business, this is mandatory.

EFINs take about 45 days to process because the IRS does a rigorous checking of each application. Prioritize getting this ID number before you start setting up your office or looking for clients. If you don't apply until November the time to get your EFIN could take longer due to volume.

In your business timeline, make sure to have your EFIN before January comes. If you file in January, you're most likely to get it by March. By that time, you won't have time to acquire clients.

Not all tax preparers need to get an EFIN. Remember, only businesses need an EFIN, not each preparer.

Chapter 3: How to Setup Your Office

Now that you're a tax preparer, you can either work for a large tax company or build your own tax preparation business. A career in tax preparation is lucrative. In 2019, both big companies and self-employed businesses contributed to the forecasted revenue of $11 billion.

There are benefits to working in a big company like H&R Block, Jackson Hewitt, or Liberty Tax. Some of the benefits are gaining valuable work experience, corporate connections, and employment stability. Of course, each company provides additional employment benefits like healthcare and bonuses.

Building your own business has its own set of benefits, too. According to FranchiseHelp.com, most are small businesses with 37% owned by single proprietors and 53% with less than 10 employees.

One of the benefits would be more freedom; especially since most work is concentrated from January until April 15 annually. It's a stable business as well since there will always be the need to pay taxes. For convenience, individuals and local businesses would rather outsource tax preparation to other firms.

If you decide to build your own business, here are some tips to get you started:
Assess your needs
Similar to any kind of business, make sure to assess first what you need to set up your business. Setting up your office would come after.

Get the necessary approvals
Start your business by acquiring the necessary registrations for it. Of course, as a tax preparer, do not forget to get your PTIN, EFIN, and business registrations. Research and talk to your local government, too. Some states and cities have additional requirements.

Create a business goal for the year

Make sure to plan your business milestones. Since you're starting out, you can set targets for at least one year.

Create a calendar to identify when you need to work on specific items for your business. As mentioned, tax preparation is busiest during the first four months of the year. Maximize the less busy season to grow your knowledge, expertise, and your business.

You can also create three-year, five-year, and ten-year plans. The clearer the business plans, the better for you.

Identify where you will work

An advantage of being a tax preparer is its mobility. You can set up your tax preparation business at home or rent an office. Many tax preparers choose to work at home. Meetings with clients could be done in co-working spaces or quiet restaurants. For privacy, a home office can accommodate clients.

However, if your home is not suitable to receive clients or do your work, renting an office space may be a better option. You can rent a small office or find a good co-working space that you can rent for longer periods of time. As your business grows, you will want to find a designated space or tax office so you can have year-round hours.

Set a budget

Of course, this is a crucial step. Building a tax preparation business has minimal start-up costs. However, that doesn't mean that you should splurge your entire budget in one go. Calculate how much you can invest and prioritize the essentials first.

Identify recurring expenses

The easiest to budget to make is the one for recurring expenses. This is the type of expense that you can easily estimate due to the schedule. Create a spreadsheet that tracks your daily, weekly, monthly, quarterly, and yearly expenses.

Here's a list of the usual recurring expenses:

Tax preparation software
PC/Laptop software programs
Continuing Education
Office Supplies (i.e., paper, envelopes, toner, etc.)
Equipment (especially those that were purchased with payment installments)
Utilities (i.e., communications, electricity, water, etc.)
Office rent
Licenses and Permits
Payroll / Employee Salary
Insurance
Tax deposits
Marketing/Advertising costs

Estimate your initial budget by reflecting on your own monthly expenses. For items or services that you do not personally use, research on its current price in the market.

Knowing your expenses per month will help you determine how much you can charge your clients. A good business stays afloat when both expenses and profits are managed well. Well, of course, having profits should be one of your goals.

Classify the type of expense over a specific period of time
If you are starting your business, it's best to create a short-term budget of three months and six months. After the timeframe you've set, check your expenses and make the necessary adjustments to your budget. Once you've gotten a hang of it, you can create your long-term budgets: one year, three years, and five years.

For fixed costs, you can create estimates for longer periods of time. However, for variable costs, you need to create estimates based on the trends you can see. In this case, reviewing your expenses every month, quarter, and year helps you get better in creating those estimates.

TIP: Find out what expenses you need to pay for one-time only. Create a separate spreadsheet so you won't be reminded to pay them at a certain schedule.

Determine how much you will charge

Now that you've outlined how much your business will cost, it's time to check how much you can charge your clients. Aside from the expenses, you also have to factor in non-variable factors such as your expertise, time, and the current market.

Most often, time and expertise are computed the same way. The idea is the higher your expertise, the faster you can get things done. However, in the tax preparation business, it's not just the speed that clients are looking after, it's also the accuracy. Additionally, the more experience you have gives you more confidence. A confident tax preparer makes the client feel better about choosing you.

Another way to determine how much you'll charge is by looking at the current market. You don't want to be undercharging or overcharging your clients because you didn't know how much clients would pay for your service. Tax preparation rates are different when you're in New York and when you're in Dallas.

Understanding the current market also means checking your competitors' rates. You don't want to be offering rates that are too low or too high from your competitors. Going too low may drive the whole market rate down. If your rates are too high, you might not get clients.

Check scenarios

Now that you have an estimate of your expenses and possible profits, it's time to build contingencies. Create "what if" scenarios to understand how much adjustments you need in your budget. Here are some questions you should ask yourself:

What if sales go up to 10%?
What if expenses double in 3 months?

What if there are unforeseen expenses?

What if your clients triple in 3 months?

What if you need to pay a penalty?

Creating these scenarios and planning contingencies to address these will help you manage your budget well.

Combine all data and create your initial budget

Once you have all the data, start creating your initial budget. Remember, you need to review and analyze your expenses and profits every month. Learning how to manage your budget will lessen the pains of maintaining and expanding your business. As time passes, creating your budget won't be as daunting as it used to be.

Essential Office Supplies

Technology has advanced and improved the way businesses are done. Even the tax industry has evolved with the emergence of tax programs and electronic filing. However, tax preparation is still an administrative type of business. So, investing in essential office supplies can ensure productivity and efficiency in your practice.

Getting Tax Forms

Most tax forms are available on the IRS website. The IRS has detailed the forms and the instructions for each one for easy download and reference. You can fill it in using the Adobe Acrobat PDF Editor. Afterward, file the forms via the e-File application.

However, not all clients want to file their tax using the IRS e-File system. Clients who opt for paper filing their tax returns do not want to take on risks on their personal tax and financial data security. Some clients may not be eligible for an e-filing option, too.

For paper filing, you can order available tax forms from the IRS for a limited quantity. Expect the forms to be mailed after ten business days. If you have regular clients who prefer paper filing, make sure to order forms as soon as you can. Tax forms for the calendar year filing are available for ordering as early as December 1 of the previous year. Paper filing is not as common as it used to so be sure to allow additional time preparing and mailing.

Example: 2021 Forms are available for ordering from December 1, 2020.

TIP: Order red ink forms from the IRS, instead of printing it on your own. Red ink forms such as Form W-2 or 1099s are specialized. If your self-printed red ink form is rejected by the IRS scanner, you will be penalized.

Where can I get paper?

When starting a business, it's better to scout for paper suppliers available in your area. Get your mail and shipping supplies from your paper suppliers, too. Shop around for your business' envelopes, mailing labels, and stationery.

The easiest way to get suppliers is through referrals. Consult with your friends and family for their recommendations.
1. Staples or Office Depot
2. Amazon
3. Costco's or Sams Club

You can also check out Paper Index's directory of paper suppliers and find one near you.

Invest in a Reliable Printer

Aside from printing tax forms, you'll be printing memos, contracts, and invoices in your business. So, a printer is one office equipment that you need to invest in. As a tax preparer, you'll be printing possibly thousands of tax forms for a year. A basic tax return with multiple schedules would be printed on a minimum of 12 pages. A bank product could easily print over 40 pages. If you are mailing any returns, you will have many more pages so the return can be mailed in. Additionally, no matter what printer you settle on, be sure to have a backup toner cartridge.

What printer should I get?

If you are buying a printer for your business, it's best that you choose a laser printer instead of an inkjet. Laser printers can handle heavy-duty printing tasks. While inkjet printers are best for home use where printing is done only on occasion.

Another advantage of laser printers is that it prints faster. Especially when you're working with high-volume printing, speed matters. Now, some laser printers are not great in printing images such as photos. However, this shouldn't be a problem since the nature of your business deals with only text and numbers.

Another feature that you might consider is the level of noise coming from your machine. If you work in a small room, a noisy printer could be disruptive.

You may also want to consider whether you will buy print-only or multi-function printers. Print-only printers provide more efficiency since the whole device is dedicated to one task only. However, multi-function printers provide a wide range of versatility for your basic office needs like printing, copying, and scanning. Choose one which best suits your needs.

Get a Reliable Laptop

All mobile businesses need a laptop. This is one of the pieces of equipment that each tax preparer should invest in. Various transactions are conducted daily through the use of the laptop: emails, purchasing of equipment or supplies, and marketing.

In the tax preparation business, having a laptop or desktop is mandatory. You would need it to keep records of your clients, prepare their taxes, and file those in the IRS e-File system.

What type of laptop should I get?

Not all laptops are created equal. So, it's important that you know what specifications you need for your business. Budget is also a big factor. Getting the right laptop would mean finding one the fits your needs without overpaying for it.

The first consideration when buying a laptop or desktop for your tax preparation business is matching the required specifications of your tax preparation software. Preparing taxes will be more difficult if your laptop is not suited to your software.

The second consideration is the amount of software you need for your business. Maybe you need a laptop that matches your Point-of-Sale (POS) device. Maybe you need one that can store your client's large financial data. Identify the programs and amount of storage you need so you can fit the laptop's specifications to it.

Without other considerations, an ideal laptop or desktop should have at least an Intel i5 processor or equivalent. It should also have at least 4GB RAM and 256GB solid-state drive (SSD). These minimum specifications guarantee that your tax preparation software and other extra programs will run smoothly.

Find the Best Tax Software
Professional tax software is the core of any tax preparation business. Purchasing one is non-negotiable if you would like your practice to perform at the optimum level.

What makes professional tax software great?
There is a lot of professional tax software available in the market. All of them provide the same output: your client's tax returns. Despite this, there are many factors to consider when choosing professional tax software.

Ease of Use

Accuracy is essential when you are in putting your client's financial data. Ideal professional tax software should be user-friendly, which would lessen possible inaccuracies that could be from a misclick of a button.

So, how would you know if your tax program is user-friendly? Well, it has to have an intuitive user interface. This means any essential button or function should be available from the launching of the program. An example of this would have a quick access menu for all of the system's features.

Aside from the professional tax software's user interface, how it's accessed is also essential. Is the tax program only available as a desktop application? An excellent tax program would have a web-based application (aside from the desktop application) that you can easily access outside of your office. A web-based application can be handy for any last-minute revisions to your client's tax forms. Web-based applications have grown in popularity since they can be so secure and the updates happen without user intervention.

PC/Mac Compatibility

Choose professional tax software that is compatible with different kinds of operating systems. It's better to plan and consider the longevity of your tax program. Advancements in technology have been faster in the past decades. You may suddenly choose to change your Microsoft OS PC to a Mac. Migrating data systems is always a pain. Lessen the possibility of having delays or missing crucial data when you choose professional tax software that works well with both Mac and PC. Most professional tax programs are Windows-based unless you use an online platform.

Type of Data Entry

Another key feature related to convenience is the data entry modes your professional tax software has. Most of the professional tax software has a "Form" data entry. In the program, you will be shown the editable tax form and then fill in the form as you would manually. Although it is practical to go through each detail line per line, it could take a lot of time.

Tax Forms and Tax Filing Availability

The ideal professional tax software must be equipped with all the federal and state tax forms. Your business relies on it! It wouldn't be convenient if you have separate tax programs for your federal and state filing.

E-filing capacity

Most professional tax software has limited e-filing features. Depending on your subscription, you may only file tax returns up to a certain number. An ideal tax program would let you file as many tax returns as you can. When you're starting your business, you may think having limited e-filing access is okay. However, as you expand your practice and acquire more clients, it would be ideal to be able to file as many tax forms as you can.

For those tax programs that have limited e-filing access, if you go beyond the allowed volume, you have to pay a different fee. In the long run, this may not be cost-efficient for your business. Find a professional tax software that has unlimited e-filing included in your subscription so you won't have to lose opportunities of getting more clients.

Customer Service

When you're a new tax preparer, learning all the tips and tricks on your new professional tax software may not come as easy. Easy-to-understand manuals and guides should be readily available to you. Better yet, a friendly customer agent could be available to help you navigate through it.

When there's a new update on the program or with the IRS, there's a need to discuss the update with someone so you can fully understand it. Asking for advice from your tax software agents is a great bonus! You'll be assured that you'll get enough support to serve your clients better.

Budget-friendly

Last but not least, excellent professional tax software must be budget-friendly. Your budget may be the most crucial factor when you're starting your tax preparation business. Of course, this does not mean you will purchase the cheapest tax program you could find. No, you must find professional tax software that brings equal value to its price. Remember, the professional tax software that you choose would be the core of your business. The ideal professional tax software would be one that has all the features you need at an affordable price.

The Best Tax Software for a Tax Preparation Business

The Best Tax Software for a Tax Preparation Business
Carter Capital Pro is the best professional tax software for both new and seasoned tax preparers. Its features and services check off on all the factors that make tax software great.

* Ease of Use Carter Capital Pro provides easy-to-use software. Its default screen offers a series of icons on its toolbar at the top of the application. These icons have been placed for the most used items. You can choose frequently used links and shortcuts for better navigation. Carter Capital Pro also populates tax forms easily from saved data on the program. You won't have to constantly request for previous data from your clients. Whatever data was saved from your previous meetings, you can easily populate it on different tax forms available on the program. Plus, and Carter Capital Pro has both English and Spanish versions. Set the program to the language you are most comfortable with. Carter Capital Pro also has an e-Signature feature. No need for your clients to travel all the way to your office to meet you to sign in. It delivers services with convenience in mind for you and your clients. Another great feature is its web-based application. You can access Carter Capital Pro Tax's professional tax software by installing on your desktop or accessing it via the internet. This is a great feature if you prepare taxes from multiple places. Additionally, Carter Capital Pro has on boarding to assist you in your initial setup.

* PC/Mac Compatibility No needs to worry about your hardware and software compatibility. Carter Capital Pro is compatible with both Microsoft and Apple OS. Use Carter Capital Pro Desktop 1040 with your Microsoft Windows OS. If you have a Mac or Chrome book, use the Carter Capital Pro Online 1040. Carter Capital Pro desktop version can be installed on many workstations that are on the same network. During the start of your tax preparation practice, you

may only need one desktop version. But as your practice grows, you may need to install more professional tax software on your employee's workstations. Carter Capital Pro does not require any additional fee for installing it. You can even save all tax returns you've prepared on your computer server for better data privacy and accessibility. Plus, for Carter Capital Pro Online 1040, updates on the tax programs are automatically downloaded and sync to your devices — no need to waste your time in downloading and installing updates. Overall ease of use, Carter Capital Pro provides great value.

* Type of Data Entry Yes, that's right. Carter Capital Pro has both the "Form" and "Interview" data entry modes. Using the "Interview" data entry mode makes it easier for both you and your client to fill in all types of tax forms. Once you've saved the data, you can quickly load all details in the tax form that you need. Building rapport with your client is essential when you're doing business. Using the "Interview" mode, you can ask for your client's details per category instead of per line in the tax form. Your questions won't be awkward because of its natural progression. If you're more familiar with the tax forms; you can choose the "Form" mode, instead. Either way, Carter Capital Pro is flexible to make filling in data more convenient for you.

* Tax Forms and Tax Filing Accessibility Carter Capital Pro is updated with all of the IRS' new tax forms. You can be assured that all of the tax forms prepared using the program complies with IRS standards. This goes for both federal and state tax forms. Yes, Carter Capital Pro is compatible with e-filing in all states.* *When using any Carter Capital Pro package*

* E-filing capacity Another Carter Capital Pro great feature is its unlimited e-filing capacity. If you choose Carter Capital Pro you can offer e-filing to all of your clients, no matter the number. Expand your business and acquire more clients without incurring additional fees! Carter Capital Pro's unlimited e-filing feature even applies to your client's back taxes. It also applies to any tax return extension your client would ask.

* Customer Service Carter Capital prides itself on providing the best customer support for its customers. A knowledge base is set up so you can be updated with the latest trends in the industry. You also receive emails relevant to the tax industry. From April to October, Carter Capital Pro offers one-on-one assistance; too. Training videos and FAQs are readily available to help anyone use the program. You may even do practice returns to get yourself familiar with the program before dealing with any client. For first-timers, a setup assistant would be available to help you with the installation. A dedicated 365 Service Phone Number is available for any of your inquiries. Gets assistance using their toll-free phone support. During critical months, customer support is also available for extended hours. Not available for calls at the moment? Contact Carter Capital via email or chat, too.

* Budget-friendly

* Carter Capital Pro has four products (New Orleans Themed) the Day Party is the Starter plan for tax preparers with little to no experience, Second Line Plan caters to tax preparers with at least one year experience and 30 min prior year returns, Mardi Gras plan is for our seasoned tax preparers with 60 min prior year returns, and our Essence Plan is geared to seasoned tax professionals looking to grow or build a team. Each product is valued at different prices to fit any tax preparer's budget and level of expertise.

Chapter 4: Setting Up Your Business Tools

Beyond the equipment you need for your business, you also need some essentials such as a business phone and business email. Both existing and new clients need to be able to reach your office to do business with you.

When you're setting up a new business, it's tempting to use your personal phone and email at the start. Do NOT do this. Although it may seem cost-efficient, there are many reasons why you should invest in your own office infrastructure.

Why should you invest in your business tools?

Providing the best customer experience

Investing in tools such as your office's phone, email, and cards means investing in your customer experience. Having dedicated tools such as a 1-800 hotline or @yourdomain.com email address provides a good customer experience.

Clients, nowadays, have many options and discern everything about the company or service provider before deciding to do business with them. Clients always check a business's website, email, and phone number. If any of your company tools are personal, they won't choose to do business with you.

Communicating with you through your business tools reiterates to your clients that you are a legitimate business. This also inspires confidence in your new business.

Preparing for future manpower growth

When you start your new tax preparation business, you might start with only a few staff members. In some cases, you only start with yourself on the payroll. However, this does not mean you don't have to invest in setting up your business tools.

When you've started expanding and hiring more staff, you would want to make sure that your tools are capable to accommodate the increase in usage. By this time, your business cannot afford to slow down. Thus, you need to make sure your tools are ready and available so your staff can work and contribute right away.

Having your own company's tools also helps your staff to gain a sense of company identity, too. Getting their own business emails gives them the confidence to communicate with clients. Especially for staff related to sales! Business cards are top priority; so they can establish their reputation as part of your company.

Investing in your brand

Aside from customer and staff usability, investing in your business tools can help build your company image. Similar to picking out your business name, you need to have the right tools that send the same message to your potential clients.

Brand awareness is when people and potential clients know about your business through simply your name. If you have your own 1-800 phone line or @yourdomain.com tools, you can easily establish brand recall for your tax business.

As pointed out, clients look for stability and reliability in companies that they would trust. Having your own phone, email, and cards can contribute to that. In the client's perspective, you have invested in your business, and therefore will not fold up shop in a moment's notice.

All in all, getting a monthly subscription for your phone line and email helps build your reputation, allows you to grow your business, and helps your clients to trust you. Now, let's find out where can you get these tools.

Business Phone

The first tool you should get is a business phone. A business phone helps with client communication. More than that, it also helps when building relationships with them.

If you are going to hire staff for your new business, the first one you would hire would be a receptionist. The receptionist can help handle calls, emails, and meeting schedules.

Separating your business phone from your personal phone also helps you build privacy. At the end of the business day, you can switch off your phone and let the machines take your clients' calls.

TIP: If you have reasonably good internet service, get a VOIP or Voice Over Internet Protocol service. They offer a wide range of services and cheaper rates. Plus, you won't need to have a separate service for your internet and your phone line.

Here are some VOIP and phone services to consider:

Skype

Skype is well-known for its free chat and call service. However, you can get a local number and set it up as your business phone. You can answer incoming calls and make outgoing calls using the Skype app from any device. Skype has a monthly, 3-month, and 12-month subscription that range from $6 to $54.

Packed with all the features of Skype free calls, you can have voicemails, call routing, video and audio calls, screen sharing, and encrypted calls. Sending files and conducting conference calls are also easy.

Plus, you can do a Search within conversations; get Call Forwarding, Voicemail, Caller ID, and Skype to Go. Another advantage of having Skype is the seamless integration with all Microsoft apps such as Office 365 and Outlook.

Phone.com

Phone.com is a cloud-based VOIP system that connects your phone system to whatever device you have, as long as it's connected to the internet. It's available in three price points with their Base ($12.99/mo), Plus ($19.99/mo), and Pro ($39.99/mo) packages for their pay-per-minute plans. They also have unlimited minutes plans ranging from $29.99 to $59.99 per month.

Used by thousands of small businesses in the U.S., Phone.com has established a good reputation based on their system's features. Standard features include Account Management, Caller ID for incoming and outgoing calls, Toll-Free Phone numbers, Voicemail, and User Extensions.

You can pick from thousands of available local, toll-free, and international numbers. You can also customize phone numbers for an additional fee. If you already have a phone number that you'd like to turn into a business phone line, you can transfer it to Phone.com using their Number Porting feature.

Set up call handling rules such as call menus or auto-attendant, call forwarding, and call transfer to help direct your clients to the right person for their concerns. Your clients will also hear soothing hold music when they're waiting for you or your staff to pick up.

Citrix Grasshopper

Grasshopper is another VOIP service that caters to small and medium businesses. In 2016, it was acquired by Citrix, which helped strengthen their service. It has three packages: the Solo, Partner, and Small Business. Their packages start from $26 to $80 per month.

Grasshopper's main strength lies in its features. Their Solo package has 1 number with 3 extensions available. Aside from that, all packages have Mobile and Desktop applications, Custom Greetings, Simultaneous Call Handling, Incoming Call Control, Call Transfers, and Instant Response. On top of these features, you also get unlimited minutes whichever plan you choose!

Another great feature that Grasshopper has is that you can get notifications via the mobile and desktop apps included. Voicemail messages are also directly encoded and sent to your mobile and email. That way, you can read and review your voicemails.

Mighty Call

Also a VOIP service, Mighty Call provides toll-free, local, and customized numbers for its clients. Having a customized number is perfect for the marketing aspect of your business. Incorporate your business name on your number or get a clever one that everyone can immediately remember.

Mighty Call's Basic package is $19.99 per month. It includes 1,000 minutes, 2 toll-free or local numbers, and 10 clients in the Contact Book. If you need unlimited minutes, you can get the Standard package available at $39.99 per month. Aside from unlimited minutes, you get additional features like Call Recording, Voice to Text, Presence Indicator, and 5 toll-free or local numbers.

What's great with Mighty Call is that all its packages include unlimited users. When you start hiring more staff, you won't have to spend additional fees to provide access to them. Mighty Call also has a desktop app with a multichannel activity dashboard that displays messages, calls, emails, and callback requests.

Business Email
One of the most essential tools you need is your business email. All correspondence to your clients and IRS will be done by email.

There is a lot of free email hosting service available now. However, not all can provide you with the data security you need. Plus, email hosts are competitive now, offering more robust features for your business.

Here are some email hosting services to consider:

Microsoft 365 for business

Microsoft 365 for Business is similar to GSuite's features. The Office 365 Business Premium plan has 50GB mailbox storage for $12.50 a month. You also get 1TB file-sharing storage via OneDrive.

You also get access to Microsoft Office tools like Excel, Word, and Powerpoint. For their communication package, you can get your Skype and Microsoft Teams. All of these features are available on your workstation and your mobile.

If you don't need to install these features on your laptop, you can opt for their all-mobile version for only $5 a month.

In terms of branding, you can get your domain name on your email addresses. Having your own "@brand.com" showcases professionalism and builds reputation.

This is a highly recommended option when building your own tax preparation business. Aside from email, having Office 365 with Microsoft Word and Excel is a necessity in the tax industry. If you're using Office 365 Business Essentials, just add $ from $7.50 per month to get the Office 365 Business Premium package.

GSuite

GSuite is a more feature-packed service of the free Gmail that we know. For only $12 a month, you can get unlimited storage, 24/7 customer support, mobile device management and security, and your own company at the email address.

Aside from the email service, you also get access to Google's other features like GDrive, Calendar, Photos, Hangouts Chat, and GDocs like Sheets, Forms, and Docs. What's great is the GSuite is compatible with all device types. You can work from your laptop to your phone within seconds.

If you need too much storage space, you can get GSuite's Basic package for $5 a month with 30GB storage space.

Rackspace

Rackspace is email hosting that's known for their robust customer service package. Support is available in 10 global centers with 3,000 cloud engineers on-standby if there's any trouble with the email hosting service.

Rackspace offers professional email hosting with your own company email address for $2.99 per month, per user. You will get Outlook, webmail, and mobile access with 25GB mailbox storage space. You also get unlimited aliases and group lists.

ZohoMail

If you don't need too much storage space or extra features, you can get Zohomail's email hosting service for only $1 per month, per user. It comes with email hosting for multiple domains, mobile app, and business calendar functions.

You can also opt for their $3 per month, per user plan that includes online file manager, instant chat communication app, and online meeting software. You also get access to tools like Wordprocessor, Spreadsheet, and Presentation software.

Business Cards
Business cards are good tools for when you are networking. Market your business by participating in trade shows and conferences. When you're in a trade show, business cards are a good way for you to give to potential clients. Now that you have your business phone and email, you can put that info on your business cards.

Despite this, this is not a critical tool that you should spend a lot of time or money on. You may end up spending a lot of money if you choose to get the design and printing of your cards professionally done.

Going to a trade show to market your business is not going to be your first marketing strategy. For your first few weeks, you can create a simple business card on your laptop and print out a few copies.

Otherwise, you can get your business cards from Vistaprint. From time to time, Vistaprint offers free design and printing of business cards, which means you only pay for shipping! If their promo is not available, you can still get free shipping from Vistaprint, which lessens your costs.

The best time to invest in business cards is when you're going to trade shows and other events that'll give you the opportunity to network. To lower costs, you can get business cards in bulk. If you have more client-facing staff, getting business cards for them in one-go can be cost-effective.

Chapter 5: Outsourced Suppliers

When you start a business, you don't have to hire a lot of professionals to work for you immediately. Having everything set up in one-go takes time and a lot of money.

For small businesses, it's highly recommended to outsource services that are not in your field of work yet. The main goal is to work on your businesses' core services and strengthen it. In this case, work on the essentials of your tax preparations' services: acquiring clients, setting up your tax software, understanding the market, and expanding into other tax-related services.

Whether you have a home office or your own commercial space, you can outsource services like shredding services, computer IT, and printing services.

Internet Service Provider (ISP)
In today's market, there's no business that does not deal with the internet. You use the internet to connect with your clients using email and messaging services. Banking and marketing are also done on the internet nowadays. Most importantly, you use the internet to file your clients' tax returns via UltimateTax.

What kind of internet service do I need?
In some towns, there's only one ISP. In others, you have different ISP options. When it comes to internet service providers, it all depends on your location.

Whether you only have one ISP option or you have several, choosing the right internet speed is what's crucial to your new tax preparation business. According to the IRS, it's recommended to have a high-speed internet connection for eFiling.

Aside from the upload and download speed, make sure the ISP you will choose has excellent customer service. Your tax software and e-File transmissions rely on good internet service. When your internet goes down, you want to be able to talk to someone from your ISP that you can count on.

TIP: Since most of your transactions will be done online, it's best to find a good and reliable ISP. Make sure to consult with your friends on a good ISP within the area. Also, find out recommendations from small business owners near your office or home.

IT Services

Any business now needs IT services. However, when you're starting, you may not need a large amount of IT support. Prioritizing which services you need first is the key to maximizing your ROI with a small budget.

Work Station & Equipment Set-Up

Beyond purchasing your laptop or desktop, you would need IT support to install the necessary applications to get it working. Your retailer would probably install the basic applications, such as your device's operating system.

Now, what about the other applications you need? There's your Microsoft Office or your iWork Suite. You also need your communication tools: Skype, WhatsApp, Outlook, Microsoft Teams, and Slack.

You would also need to install any of your equipment's software. You need to make sure your printer and scanner are connected. Eventually, you would also get your data server to have better data security. You have to make sure all your devices are connected to the internet for maximum efficiency.

Great news! You don't have to worry too much about your tax software installation with UltimateTax. Our customer service will help you through the installation. Our customer support will help you with any problems related to Carter Capital, all-year-round. Carter Capital Pro also has many support articles on installing.

If you only have one workstation to work on, you can do this by yourself. However, it takes time. It takes more time if you are not very adept with today's technology. That's working time you could spend finding new clients and working to build your brand and reputation.

Marketing services

Another service that you could outsource is your part of your marketing strategy. An advantage of outsourcing marketing services is that you won't have to pay the cost of hiring a full-time employee. Plus, you get to work with experts in the industry.

You may still handle other marketing aspects of your business, such as marketing events and face-to-face meet-ups with your target market. However, you can delegate your digital marketing to a third party company. Here are some marketing aspects that you can already outsource:

Logo and Brands

Unless you already have a specific idea of what your logo and brand would be, you can outsource and hire a graphic artist to render it all. A better idea would be for you to share those ideas with your graphic artist and let him make it visual or improve on it.

Depending on the graphic artist's rates and agreed work, you'll get at least three options for your logo and brands. You can further discuss revisions to get the logo you want.

Remember, your logo is also crucial to your marketing. It'll be part of your business cards, official stationery, and ads. So, when you choose the graphic artist that will handle your logos, make sure you've already checked his previous works. You need to find someone whose visual style resonates with yours.

Keep in mind your target market, too. Tax preparation is a serious and professional business. Do you think the previous works of the graphic artist shows this kind of professionalism? You'll need to partner with an artist that can get this message across through design.

Website Design

Nowadays, your website is equal to your business card. If a client wants to know more about your business, she will look at your website. If you don't have a website, the client may think twice about the legitimacy of your business.

Unless you are a former web developer, building a reliable website is not easy. Instead of spending hours figuring out how to work on multiple codes to make one, hire a company that does website design.

Browse for companies (or freelancers) that offer this type of service. Find out what services they provide and their rates.

Also, browse through their portfolio. Find out what websites they've made. You'll soon find out that most of their website design has a certain feel or look. You can decide whether that feel or look fits your business' design.

Web Marketing Services

Now that you have your website and your logo design, you should consider getting help to run your web marketing. The next step, in terms of marketing, is getting customers to click on your website.

This is where Search Engine Optimization (SEO) comes in. It's the process of getting quality and quantity of web traffic into your website using keywords. The goal is that when someone googles "tax preparer" or "tax preparation near me," your website becomes one of the top results.

Once your website is one of the top results, there's a big percentage that a client will click on it and learn more about you. Now, your website must sell your tax expertise and convince the client to hire you as a tax preparer. Web marketing services take care of the SEO of your website, so you can get more clients to hire you.

Chapter 6: Investing in Your Own Office Space

Getting an office is a very big decision to make. As a new tax preparer starting a business, you need to weigh in both the positive and negative before renting (or buying!) your own office space.

An advantage of starting a tax preparation business is that you can start it in your home office. As long as you have enough space to accommodate your clients for meetings, you can start at the comfort of your home.

However, you need to also remember that having an office lends credibility to your business. A client will trust you and do business with you when they can see that you work in a professional and respectable place.

What to Consider When Deciding on Investing in Your Office Space?

Budget

Of course, the first to consider is whether you have a budget for an office. Consider the capital you are willing to invest in your new business first.

When you invest in your office space, you should be ready for a full commitment. You need to ensure you have a budget for at least a year. In some cities, you can rent for a minimum of six months. These are still substantial costs for your start-up business.

About 23% of commercial space owners expect an increase in their rates in 2020 as they continue to upgrade their properties to 'smart buildings.' Even though you are not looking for office spaces in smart buildings, this surge in rental rates can affect the overall commercial real estate market.

When it comes to the rental price, you also have to factor in where you will do your business.

Remember, an office rental rate is also indicative of how much you should charge for your services in your location's target market. If you choose to get an office in the high-end part of your town, you'll also need to charge expensive rates. If you get an affordable office, you can charge less.

Location, Location, Location

A big factor in the increase or decrease in rental rates is the location. Even if you are not building your business in major cities, rental rates will vary depending on the location you choose. Is it in the posh and influential part of town? That's going to be expensive. How about getting an office downtown?

Aside from rental rates, you also need to find a location that's fit for your tax business. Consider the reputation of your chosen location for your office. Make sure your office is not near shops or offices that have a problematic reputation. Also, since you will be discussing financial information with your clients, you need to make sure the office space is in a quiet and secure location.

Since the tax preparation business is a service-type of business, it's best to have a storefront office in a retail shopping environment. A location that has a lot of foot traffic helps you gain more customers; especially during tax season.

You can choose an office near shops that are convenient for your clients. For example, choose a space near check-cashing, convenience stores, inner-city supermarkets, car dealerships, and loan retail shops.

Another location you can consider is in an office park. You can capture the market of employees in an office park. Most often employees would like to get their taxes done before or after work. Getting a space in an office park helps you bring convenience to your target market.

Office Size

When it comes to size, a tax preparation business does not need too much space; especially, when you're starting out.

You need to have enough room for a reception area, a private meeting room, and an area to do all your tasks. However, do not discount the possibility that you could be expanding. So, keep in mind enough space for an additional workstation or two.

In terms of office layout, make sure your meeting rooms are not near areas where there are lots of activities. When discussing your client's finances, you wouldn't want them to be distracted or feel uncomfortable. Make sure they have enough privacy.

Getting Help From Real Estate Brokers

When looking for office spaces, you can seek the help of commercial leasing agents. These agents can help you find the most suitable spaces that you may need. Some agents provide their service for free and get their profit from the commission. Others will request for a small fee in advance.

There are advantages and disadvantages to getting help from commercial listing agents or real estate brokers. Some of the advantages are:

Guidance from an expert; especially when it comes to leasing agreements
Additional help in facilitating negotiations to your lease
Advance knowledge of spaces or properties that may not be available yet
Saves you time in finding spaces on your own

Some of the disadvantages of getting an agent are:

Showing properties that may not be the best for you in favor of a higher commission
Not having enough listings to get you a property that fits your office needs

May favor a specific property owner or landlord.

Should you choose to get the help of a real estate agent, make sure to meet with more than one? You can get different insights and additional knowledge from your discussions with different agents.

If you don't want to use a commercial listing agent, you can communicate and negotiate with property owners on your own. Nowadays, finding office spaces can be a breeze because there are lots of real estate companies that show available listings on their website. You can check out office spaces from WeWork, Regus, LoopNet, Commercial Cafe, and OfficeSpace.com. You can also check out the websites of the local real estate companies in your area.

Chapter 7: Acquiring Your Clients

After setting up your office, it's time to work on your business strategy in getting clients. As a new tax preparer, you need to establish trust among your peers and potential clients. Aside from that, you need to build a good reputation when it comes to providing services.

So, the next question is, how do you start acquiring clients?

Market Your Business
Before talking to any potential clients, you must have developed marketing tools that are ready to use.

Create Your Brand
Your brand defines the essence of your business. Establishing your business' brand is essential when it comes to marketing it. It's a communication tool from your company to your existing and potential clients about your products and services. It relays what customers should expect from your business.

So, your business' brand is more than your logo, store design, or even your product. It has to communicate what your business is committing.

For a tax preparation business, what commitments should you highlight?

High Accuracy Rate
Commitment to Deadlines
Trustworthy
Transparency and Reliability
Credible (i.e., member or affiliate of organizations, certified by IRS)
Excellent customer service (i.e., businesses who can handle your questions even after the filing season is over)
Quick action

Consider the descriptions above. Identify which ones you want to emphasize. Aside from that, reflect on what makes your business different from the others. Knowing what processes you do differently can be a good thing to highlight against the competition.

Set a Targeted Audience

Knowing your market is crucial for when you do marketing for your new tax preparation business. If you know your target audience, you will be able to set the tone of your marketing strategies. For example, what type of marketing language or tactics you need for clients who are employed and filing their income tax? How about for clients who own small businesses?

Find out what clients value when it comes to tax preparation in your area. For example, they value accuracy and reliability. They may also appreciate excellent and accessible communication about their taxes since most of them would not be experts. It's better to focus your marketing messages on your skills in helping your clients understand their taxes.

For corporations and big businesses, you may want to learn more about each business's niche or specialization. This may take time. So, most often, tax preparers who work with corporations choose to specialize in specific industries. For example, a tax preparation company may solely work on manufacturing companies, and another would specialize in restaurant businesses. In this case, you can highlight your company's expertise when you know your target audience.

Remember, you must be aware of what type of tax preparation services you'd offer your clients. Based on the type of tax returns that you will specialize, you can identify who are your primary clients.

Use a channel for engagement

Once you've identified your brand and narrowed down your target audience, you need to plan how you will communicate those effectively.

Build an online presence

Nowadays, both small and big businesses need a website. Consumers have adapted to the digital age. In 2019, 97% of consumers go online to find local businesses instead of printed directories.

Websites help in communicating your products and services to a wide range of clients. When someone needs a service, most often, they will Google and find a company for it. Aside from that, a website is an excellent tool to showcase your products and services. It also helps your clients find and contact your office. A good website will communicate to your customers what services you offer. It's also a good venue for them to contact you and book an appointment.

Building a good reputation in your online profile is also an excellent way to attract new customers. Existing clients could share testimonials and online reviews. According to a survey by Dimensional Research, 90% claimed that reading positive online reviews influenced their decisions to purchase a product or service.

Search Engine Optimization (SEO) works well in building your website's online presence. Consider outsourcing web marketing services so you could get into the top search results when clients try to find businesses related to tax preparation.

Use traditional marketing tools

A good way to market your new tax preparation business is also to use traditional marketing tools. Despite being in the digital age, traditional marketing strategies still work; especially for businesses centered in service like tax preparation. It works because taxes, although generic, are always personal. So, when looking for clients, you need also to use tools that have specific personal touches.

Business cards

Business cards are still crucial to marketing any business. Giving your business card to a potential client is personal and professional. Distribute them in a networking event, conferences, local restaurants, laundry mats, or at a party. Anytime you meet a potential client; you can readily give information and make a business connection.

Networking Events & Conferences

Attending conferences and meeting people is an excellent way to market your tax preparation business. When it comes to providing services, getting one-on-one time with potential clients make more significant impacts.

Take note: do not expect to market your tax preparation business in IRS conferences. Instead, go to conferences where your clients are. Is your target market small businesses? Attend franchise expos or Chamber of Commerce meetings. You should also join the Chamber of Commerce's after-hours events or breakfast meetings. Join local groups and get to know other members, too.

When available, volunteer or sign up to be one of the event's speakers. It's a great opportunity for you to showcase your expertise and bring interest to your business.

Giveaways

Investing in giveaway items is useful for when you attend networking events or conferences related to your industry. These items help you become top of mind when tax season comes.

Direct Mail

Send out a postcard to remind potential clients that tax season is coming. A potential client would appreciate the reminder and check out your business.

Develop promos and incentives
Whether you're acquiring first clients or wanting to add some more to your current roster, developing promos can drive interest to your company. Consumers show a lot of interest when they're told that they can save money. Give an incentive for clients who does early tax filing. If you offer bank products, try a limited-time offer discount.

However, when it comes to promos, do not limit yourself with tax-related items either. Think outside the box. Dealing with taxes is often stressful; so, why not raffle off a day at the spa for your clients?

Run promos and incentives to get your clients interested, and then deliver exceptional service so they'd stay.

Client Acquisition
Now that you've established the marketing tools that you'll use, you can focus more on targeting potential clients.

First clients: Family and Friends
The first clients you should consider acquiring are your family and friends. Why? It's because you have established trust and a good reputation with them even before you've approached them to offer your services.

Building a tax preparation business is all about service. The biggest hurdle of acquiring clients is establishing trust. With your family and friends as clients, you won't have to worry about it. Instead, you can focus on providing excellent service, which your clients could rave about. Offering your service to friends and family is a good way to start to develop your own process. All successful businesses are built on established and effective processes.

Another benefit of having your friends and family as your first clients is the feedback that you can receive for your services. There won't be any hesitation from you or your client to share what was good and bad from your transactions. Their feedback will help you improve your services, which you could advertise to get more clients.

So, how do you ask your friends and family to be your clients? Look into your immediate circle of influence. Contact your Church members, organizations, school friends, and relatives. Reach out to them and share that you are starting your own tax preparation business.

For those who are employed, offer to prepare their income tax returns. If you know anyone who has a business, you can offer to process their Tax Form 1040's. If you already have a business and would want to expand it by adding a tax preparation service, reach out to your existing clients. You can also offer to prepare 1099s for their businesses, too.

How to convert your friends into clients?

There are four types of people that we know: acquaintances, proximity friends, close friends and family or relatives. All of them are potential clients. Now, what's important is to understand how you could approach them to convert them into your business' clients.

Acquaintances

There's great potential in marketing when you meet someone for the first time. Most often, people you just met would have conversations about basic information like where you grew up or what do you do. Steer your conversation about your business to inform your acquaintance of your services. Casually share the services you offer and establish your expertise during the conversation.

Sometimes, acquaintances do not want to talk about business throughout the conversation, especially if you are not in a business or networking setting. In this case, it's better not to dive into your business first-hand. Get to know the person's needs first.

Proximity Friends

Friends, you know from work or your commute but do not have enough connections, are called proximity friends. These are the people you say hello and chat briefly on the train or in the supermarket. Since you do not have similar interests, how do you broach the subject of asking them to be in business?

A good way to introduce your business is by striking up a conversation about a general problem related to your business. Identify the issues your friend is having with their existing provider.

Relate to them and share the difficulties you've encountered about preparing your taxes previously. Emphasize how you found a solution that you apply via your business. Make sure to give your business card after your conversation.

After your conversation, invite your friend out to lunch so you could talk more about how you can help them. This way, you can establish more rapport and build a deeper relationship with them.

Close Friends

Having conversations with your close friends is easy since you've developed trust and connection over time. They are the kind of friends who you've shared interests, and you've spent significant events in your life with them. In this case, asking for their help in your business all about timing.

Share your business during the planning stages. Seek advice from them about small details. Afterward, ask them to consider using your services to help with your business.

When you ask them, make sure to emphasize how good you are with your work. Remind them how you are an expert in your field. Give examples of when they were able to witness (first-hand) how you value your work.

However, be mindful of how you ask your close friends. Don't pressure them into doing business with you. If they turn you down, ask them to remember you when they change their minds.

Family or Relatives

Your family and relatives may be the easiest to ask for support. Offer them your services, such as working on their income tax returns. If they cannot give you their business, ask them to recommend you to their friends.

Once you've converted your friends and families as clients, deliver the quality of service you've promised them. Don't be complacent that since you already have a personal relationship with them, you won't treat them like a real customer. The key to building a good reputation is making sure you do an exceptional job that your clients, whoever they may be.

Referral from existing clients

After building a good working relationship within your immediate circle of influence, the next step is to acquire clients through referrals. Your current clients could vouch for your excellent work. Then, they could recommend you to their family and friends.

Your previous clients' testimonies are valuable to the marketing of your services to new potential clients.

Word-of-mouth marketing is still the most reliable type of marketing for consumers.

One more benefit of acquiring clients through referrals is its cost-effectiveness. Your primary investment is providing excellent service to your previous clients. One that would be impressive enough for them to start talking about you to others.

Now, all you have to do is ask. Here are some of the ways on how you can ask your previous clients for referrals:

Directly ask

Once you've built a good working relationship with your clients, ask them if they could refer you to their friends and family. Better yet, ask them if they know anyone who needs your services. Ask them for referrals through email, phone calls, or in-person. You can even get creative by adding a note at the bottom of your invoices. That way, your clients can be reminded to share leads with you.

Thank your clients for previous referrals

If your clients have given you referrals, take the time to thank them. Having a tax preparation business is more than just crunching the numbers, it's about building relationships. Send a handwritten note or thank them in person. Clients most likely continue giving referrals when they know they were appreciated.

Offer incentives

Everyone likes getting a gift. Step up your thank you's through giving gifts. Whether it's a simple gift like chocolates or a gift card, your client will appreciate it. Tell your client that you'll provide an incentive for every good referral they give. Aside from wanting to recommend you to others because of your excellent service, they'll also be motivated by the gift they'll receive in return.

Create a referral program

Give your existing clients a chance to earn by setting up a referral program. It may be similar to offering incentives, but in this case, you can offer a percentage of a successful sale. You can also provide discounts on your services when a client's referral uses your services, too.

Your clients will be motivated, not only to submit referrals but also to close the sale. They can help you by convincing their referrals to consider your company based on their excellent working relationship with you.

Indirect Referrals

If your clients do not have any referrals for you, ask them to for their testimonials. Ask them to share your website or leave an online review to spread the good word about your tax preparation business.

You can also ask your clients for permission to create a case study based on their transaction with you. Writing a case study shows readers how you would handle particular tax problems, which may be relevant to them. You can discuss this specific case study during conferences or write a blog on your website. Assure your clients that you won't reveal any personal information when you create one.

Marketing to Your Niche

Beyond your clients and their referrals, you can acquire clients by marketing to your niche. With both traditional and digital marketing, there are lots of ways to reach new potential clients.

Networking with Professionals

Another way to market your tax preparation business is through networking with professionals. Reach out to industries that are related to tax preparation such as insurance, real estate, and banks. Professionals within these industries have possible clients that could need your company's services. Offer them your referral program to get an introduction to key clients.

Selling Your Expertise

With a tax preparation business, you would want to show potential clients that you have the know-how to get the job done efficiently and effectively. You can achieve this through both traditional and digital marketing.

Volunteering or participating in conventions as a speaker is one way to share your know-how. You could talk about a tax problem and explain how you would solve it. If you cannot be a speaker, participate in the conference by sponsorship. Set up a booth and start talking to attendees about your tax preparation business. Try to have an "Ask Me About Taxes" booth, where attendees can come up to you and ask your questions related to tax.

Another way to showcase your know-how is through content marketing. Write a blog or create a podcast where you discuss tax topics. Find out what questions your potential clients need to know and start talking about it in forums and blogs as an expert. What's good is that you can direct those readers and listeners to your website, and they can learn more about your tax preparation business. Connect through Facebook, Instagram, and Twitter. Use popular social media sites to share your knowledge.

When tax season is near, reach out to local TV news stations or talk show and ask if they would like to do a piece on taxes. You can also reach out to radio shows and local newspapers, in case they want to do a feature on you. If you can, invest and get a paid spot on that TV segment, radio show, or newspaper feature.

A good marketing campaign is utilizing available marketing tools and strategies. Assess your market and goal to find the right tools that you can invest it. Some marketing campaigns pay off immediately, while others take time. Research and find out which ones you can do within the budget you've set.

Chapter 8: Tips for New Tax Preparers

New Tax Preparers: Employment vs. Business

People choose the tax preparation business for multiple reasons. One of which is that it's a good expansion from their current profession or trade.

High school graduates go into the tax preparation business because it is a stable and fruitful career. Anyone who wants to change their professions towards the finance industry can start with tax preparation. It's also an excellent way to get networking connections with professionals in the insurance, real state, and banking industries.

For those who've never had any tax preparation experience before, the question is always whether to seek employment first or establish your own tax preparation business. Once you've earned your Enrolled Agent status and register with the IRS, you can already start acquiring clients and provide tax preparation services. However, you can also choose to be employed as a tax preparer under H&R Block, Liberty Tax Services, or Jackson Hewitt. So, which is the best move?

Well, it all depends on your professional goals. Do you want to specialize in the preparation of income taxes? Do you want to handle tax cases for small and big businesses? Specialization of tax cases requires more knowledge and practice. Remember, there are tax cases in which tax preparers need licenses to work on them.

Starting a tax preparation business is easy. Getting the necessary documents like PTIN, EFIN, and State registrations are easy and readily available. It only requires minimal start-up capital, and you can initially work from home. But, a tax preparation business is more than just setting up your office. There are the business and the technical side of it.

The technical side is getting the necessary paperwork, learning how to do tax preparations, establishing processes, and handling of your finances. The business side is the marketing, sales, and expanding the business to keep it afloat. If you're ready to take on these responsibilities altogether, consider establishing your business soon.

If you need more training on handling one or both sides of the business, you should also consider getting employment. Being a tax preparer for big businesses exposes you to different types of clients, tax cases, and opportunities. Working in established companies can help you get the on-the-job training for your technical skills. Aside from that, you can learn to understand the business while being part of the company.

Understanding the Tax Codes is #1 priority.

As a tax preparer, you need to understand the tax codes. It's the fundamental knowledge for working in the industry. But, of course, you can't know it all. There are many various tax codes for different industries. This is where specialization comes in.

Additionally, the biggest challenge a tax preparer face is knowing where to find the information. Of course, getting regular updates straight from the IRS is ideal. Visit the IRS Tax Code, Regulations, and Official Guidance page as references to the tax codes and laws you need to be familiar with. Make sure to follow Publication 17, the official IRS publication for tax preparation on individual tax returns.

IRS also regular updates through the Publication 1345. Another reference that you need to keep checking is the IRS Circulars. Check the Circular 230, which is required by all professional tax preparers. If there is a new update from the IRS, you may want to confirm your understanding by taking continuing education courses.

If you want to continue enriching your know-how on tax codes, the IRS also offers classes under the Voluntary Annual Filing Season Program (AFSP). The program is designed to incentivize non-credentialed tax preparers. They offer Continuing Education (CE) that helps broaden your understanding of the tax code. If you chose to participate, you would need to complete 18 units of CE every year. For your convenience, you can finish your CE credits online. Work on your units at your own pace, anytime, and anywhere.

Once you complete the 18 units and pass the test, you will receive a completion certificate from the IRS. You will also be included in the tax preparer public directory. Being part of the IRS' public directory is their way of recommending you to potential clients.

Aside from the AFSP, continue learning about the tax industry by attending conferences and events. Interact and participate with other tax professionals. Listen to other tax professionals whenever they discuss their case studies. Understand their methods and analyze how you can incorporate them into your own processes.

Remember, as a tax preparer, it is your responsibility to know and be up-to-date with the tax codes. Your clients will depend on your expertise to solve their tax filing issues.

Credibility and Expertise

Build a reputation that shows off your expertise and credibility. A client needs someone who can help them navigate and understand their taxes. Gain confidence through learning the ins and outs of the tax industry; especially, the tax codes.

Honesty and Reliability

Taxes are not something that needs flash or grandiose. It's a reality that everyone needs to face. So, clients are not looking for tax preparers who simply impress them with freebies. They are looking for someone honest and reliable.

The tax season is only from January to April. However, clients sometimes need help with taxes during the off-season. A good tax preparer can be relied upon for consultations even during those times.

Clients also need honest tax preparers. If there's a problem with their taxes, clients would want to know if you can tell them straightforwardly. If there's an issue with taxes, it is better to face it head-on and immediately because there could be penalties involved. Clients would want a professional who is not afraid to inform them of the issues and come prepared with solutions.

Relate-ability and Good Customer Service

Clients also look for tax preparers that they can relate to. Apart from sharing their financial documents, clients need to discuss their financials face-to-face. Of course, most of the information is sensitive and confidential. New clients have a hard time talking about these issues with a stranger. So, a tax preparer must know how to build good rapport and relationships with clients.

Aside from being reliable, clients also look for excellent customer service. Tax cases do get complicated. Clients will ask a lot of questions. Beyond filing taxes, clients also need to know the next steps. If they get any letter from the IRS, they would need someone who can help them handle it.

Excellent customer service also does not end with tax-related issues. As simple as getting help to get your services as a tax preparer or paying for your services. These are business-related items that should be easy for your clients to deal with. If problems arise, you should be able to provide help.

Get the best tools that'll help you grow your tax business.
Once you've started your tax business, you always have to think about how it can grow. When you invest your money into buying pieces of equipment, services, or tools, you need to get the ones that'll fit your budget and still be the best one there is. The key is finding what would be a good value for your money.

This is especially important when you decide on which tax software you will purchase. You need to find reliable, accurate, and easy-to-use tax software that provides the best value for your investment. Remember, you are not just purchasing a program for your office. You are purchasing the core tool in which you will build your entire business.

There are many factors to consider when choosing your professional tax software. There's the program's price, accuracy, ease of use, and features. Aside from the program itself, you also have to find one that gives the best support.

Carter Capital has great features at the most affordable price. You can choose between its products: Day Party, Second Line, Mardi Gras, and Essence Plans. You can check each product's features to find one that fits your business the best. All of which come with Smart Diagnostics, State Modules, Context-Sensitive Help, Interview Mode Entry Forms, Easy-to-use interface with its own User LaunchPad, and Year-round Support.

Another advantage of getting Carter Capital is its bank products. You can earn more and give more solutions to your clients through bank products from trusted banks like Santa Barbara TPG and Refundo.

If you need to know more about how Carter Capital can help your business grow, check how Carter Capital fares when compared with other available tax software. You'll see how much value this professional tax software can provide to your new business. Request a free no obligation demo today!